C000018940

♏ LOVE SIGNS ♏

SCORPIO

24 October – 22 November

JULIA & DEREK PARKER

DK

DORLING KINDERSLEY
London • New York • Stuttgart • Moscow

Dedicated to Martin Lethbridge

A DORLING KINDERSLEY BOOK

Project Editor • Annabel Morgan
Art Editor • Anna Benjamin
Managing Editor • Francis Ritter
Managing Art Editor • Derek Coombes
DTP Designer • Cressida Joyce
Production Controller • Martin Croshaw

ACKNOWLEDGMENTS

Photography: Steve Gorton: pp. 10, 13–15, 17–19, 46–49; Ian O'Leary: 16. *Additional photography by:* Colin Keates, Dave King, Monique Le Luhandre, David Murray, Tim Ridley, Clive Streeter, Harry Taylor, Matthew Ward. *Artworks:* Nici Demin: 34–45; Peter Lawman: *jacket*, 4, 12; Paul Redgrave: 24–33; Satwinder Sehmi: *glyphs*; Jane Thomson: *borders*; Rosemary Woods: 11. Peter Lawman's paintings are exhibited by the Portal Gallery Ltd, London.

Picture credits: Bridgeman Art Library/Hermitage, St. Petersburg: 51; Robert Harding Picture Library: 20l, 20c, 20r; Images Colour Library: 9; The National Gallery, London: 11; Tony Stone Images: 21t, 21b; The Victoria and Albert Museum, London: 5; Zefa: 21c.

Thanks to: Sarah Ashun, Emma Brogi, Charlie Chan, John Filbey, Jane Lawrie, Sharon Lucas, Daniel McCarthy, Marion McLornan, Christine Rista, Ola Rudowska, Tim Scott, Isobel Sinden, Martha Swift, Mark Thurgood, Cangy Venables *and* Liz Wagstaff.

First published in Great Britain in 1996 by
Dorling Kindersley Limited, 9 Henrietta Street, London WC2E 8PS

A CIP catalogue record for this book is available from the British Library.

ISBN 0-7513-0334-8

Reproduced by Bright Arts, Hong Kong
Printed and bound by Imago, Hong Kong

CONTENTS

Astrology & You 8

Looking for a Lover 10

You & Your Lover 12

The Food of Love 16

Places to Love 20

Venus & Mars 22

Your Love Life 24

Your Sex Life 34

Tokens of Love 46

Your Permanent Relationship 50

Venus & Mars Tables 52

ASTROLOGY & YOU

THERE IS MUCH MORE TO ASTROLOGY THAN YOUR SUN SIGN.
A SIMPLE INVESTIGATION INTO THE POSITION OF THE OTHER
PLANETS AT THE MOMENT OF YOUR BIRTH WILL PROVIDE YOU
WITH FASCINATING INSIGHTS INTO YOUR PERSONALITY.

*Y*our birth sign, or Sun sign, is the sign of the zodiac that the Sun occupied at the moment of your birth. The majority of books on astrology concentrate only on explaining the relevance of the Sun signs. This is a simple form of astrology that can provide you with some interesting but rather general information about you and your personality. In this book, we take you a step further, and reveal how the planets Venus and Mars work in association with your Sun sign to influence your attitudes towards romance and sexuality.

In order to gain a detailed insight into your personality, a "natal" horoscope, or birth chart, is necessary. This details the position of all the planets in our solar system at the moment of your birth, not just the position of the Sun. Just as the Sun occupied one of the 12 zodiac signs when you were born, perhaps making you "a Geminian" or "a Sagittarian", so each of the other planets occupied a certain sign. Each planet governs a different area of your personality, and the planets Venus and Mars are responsible for your attitudes to love and sex respectively.

For example, if you are a Sun-sign Sagittarian, according to the attributes of the sign you should be a dynamic, freedom-loving character. However, if Venus occupied Libra when you were born, you may make rather a passive and clinging partner – qualities that are supposedly completely alien to Sagittarians.

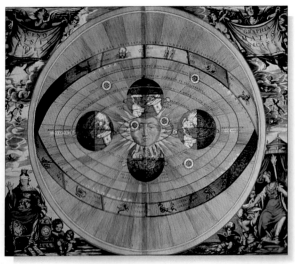

A MAP OF THE CONSTELLATION

*The 16th-century astronomer Copernicus first made the
revolutionary suggestion that the planets orbit the Sun
rather than the Earth. In this 17th-century constellation
chart, the Sun is shown at the centre of the solar system.*

The tables on pages 52–61 of
this book will enable you to
discover the positions of Mars
and Venus at the moment of
your birth. Once you have
gleaned this information, turn to
pages 22–45. On these pages we
explain how the influences of

Venus and Mars interact with
the characteristics of your
Sun sign. This information
will provide you with many
illuminating insights into your
personality, and explains how
the planets have formed your
attitudes to love and sex.

LOOKING FOR A LOVER

ASTROLOGY CAN PROVIDE YOU WITH VALUABLE INFORMATION
ON HOW TO INITIATE AND MAINTAIN RELATIONSHIPS. IT CAN
ALSO TELL YOU HOW COMPATIBLE YOU ARE WITH YOUR LOVER,
AND HOW SUCCESSFUL YOUR RELATIONSHIP IS LIKELY TO BE.

*P*eople frequently use astrology to lead into a relationship, and "What sign are you?" is often used as a conversation opener. Some people simply introduce the subject as an opening gambit, while others place great importance on this question and its answer.

Astrology can affect the way you think and behave when you are in love. It can also provide you with fascinating information about your lovers and your relationships. Astrology cannot tell you who to fall in love with, or who to avoid, but it can offer you some very helpful advice.

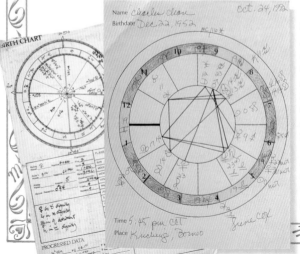

BIRTH CHARTS
*Synastry involves
the comparison
of two people's
charts in order
to assess their
compatibility in
all areas of their
relationship.
The process can
highlight any
areas of common
interest or
potential conflict.*

People whose signs are grouped under the same element tend to find it easy to fall into a happy relationship. The groupings are:

FIRE: *Aries, Leo, Sagittarius*
EARTH: *Taurus, Virgo, Capricorn*
AIR: *Gemini, Libra, Aquarius*
WATER: *Cancer, Scorpio, Pisces*

When you meet someone to whom you are attracted, astrology can provide you with a valuable insight into his or her personality. It may even reveal unattractive characteristics that your prospective partner is trying to conceal.

Astrologers are often asked to advise lovers involved in an ongoing relationship, or people who are contemplating a love affair. This important aspect of astrology is called synastry, and involves comparing the birth charts of the two people concerned. Each birth chart records the exact position of the planets at the moment and place of a person's birth.

By interpreting each chart separately, then comparing them, an astrologer can assess the compatibility of any two people, showing where problems may arise in their relationship, and where strong bonds will form.

One of the greatest astrological myths is that people of some signs are not compatible with people of certain other signs. This is completely untrue. Whatever your Sun sign, you can have a happy relationship with a person of any other sign.

YOU & YOUR LOVER

KNOWING ABOUT YOURSELF AND YOUR LOVER IS THE KEY TO
A HAPPY RELATIONSHIP. HERE WE REVEAL THE TRADITIONAL
ASSOCIATIONS OF SCORPIO, YOUR COMPATIBILITY WITH ALL THE
SUN SIGNS, AND THE FLOWERS LINKED WITH EACH SIGN.

THE HAWTHORN,
AND OTHER
BUSHY TREES,
ARE RULED
BY SCORPIO

DRAMATIC DARK
REDS AND
MAROONS ARE
TRADITIONALLY
LINKED WITH
SCORPIO

SCORPIO WAS
ONCE RULED
BY MARS,
BUT PLUTO IS
THE MODERN
RULER OF
THIS SIGN

THE GERANIUM
IS ONE OF THE
FLOWERS RULED
BY SCORPIO

INSECTS AND
CRUSTACEANS
ARE ALWAYS
ASSOCIATED
WITH SCORPIO

SCORPIOS POSSESS
A DETERMINED
STANCE AND
AN ENERGETIC,
BOUNDING GAIT

SCORPIO AND ARIES

An intense, passionate Scorpio may find an optimistic Arien too straightforward and independent. However, you share a powerful sex drive, and this should be a stormy but satisfying pairing.

Lavender is a Geminian flower

Thistles are ruled by Aries

SCORPIO AND TAURUS

The tenacious passion of Taurus will appeal to an intense Scorpio. Potentially this is a very solid match, although the jealousy of Scorpio and the possessiveness of Taurus must be kept in check.

The rose is associated with Taurus

SCORPIO AND GEMINI

You two are complete opposites. You are all passion and intensity, while Gemini is flighty and frivolous. Geminian flirtatiousness may provoke Scorpio jealousy, resulting in tempestuous scenes.

The lily, and other white flowers, are ruled by Cancer

SCORPIO AND CANCER

This is likely to be a successful pairing of two sensitive and passionate water signs. You both possess an instinctive awareness of each other's needs, and neither of you fear strong emotions.

SCORPIO AND LEO

Scorpios would like light-hearted Leos to be a little more intense, and your strong wills may do battle. However, the two of you have the potential to become a passionate and powerful couple.

*Hydrangeas
are governed by Libra*

*Sunflowers
are ruled
by Leo*

SCORPIO AND LIBRA

Librans love peace and harmony, while you relish stormy scenes and unbridled passions. However, if Libran tact can calm your turbulent emotions, this will be a satisfying and enduring match.

SCORPIO AND VIRGO

You share a serious attitude to life and are both purposeful and determined. Allow your Scorpio passions slowly to awaken Virgoan sensuality, and this will be a happy and rewarding alliance.

*Honeysuckle is
attributed to Scorpio*

*Small, brightly-coloured flowers
are associated with Virgo*

SCORPIO AND SCORPIO

This is the archetypal love-hate relationship. You are both jealous and resentful, but the pair of you are also loyal, loving, and passionate. This will be a stormy, but sexy, and very solid, alliance.

SCORPIO AND SAGITTARIUS
The cheerful, carefree attitude of
Sagittarius is completely alien to
an intense and passionate Scorpio.
However, opposites do attract,
and you may find the optimism
of Sagittarius refreshing.

*Orchids are
associated
with
Aquarius*

*Carnations
are ruled by
Sagittarius*

SCORPIO AND AQUARIUS
The cool glamour of Aquarius
will bowl you over, but their
love of freedom and lack of
emotion will disappoint a
passionate Scorpio. However, this
could be a stimulating match.

SCORPIO AND CAPRICORN
Capricornian determination will
attract you, but you may find
them too unemotional. However,
if you awaken the earthy passions
beneath the cool exterior, this
could be a sensual combination.

*Viburnum
is governed
by Pisces*

*Pansies are
Capricornian
flowers*

SCORPIO AND PISCES
Piscean emotions run just as
deep as Scorpio passions. Have
patience, and you will bring out
all the best Piscean qualities, but
be gentle, for sensitive, dreamy
Pisceans are easily hurt.

THE FOOD OF LOVE

WHEN PLANNING A SEDUCTION, THE SENSUOUS DELIGHTS OF AN
EXQUISITE MEAL SHOULD NEVER BE UNDERESTIMATED. READ ON
TO DISCOVER THE PERFECT MEAL FOR EACH OF THE SUN SIGNS,
GUARANTEED TO AROUSE INTEREST AND STIR DESIRE.

*Scorpios will
relish the sharp,
tangy flavour and
velvety texture of rich
blackcurrant fool.*

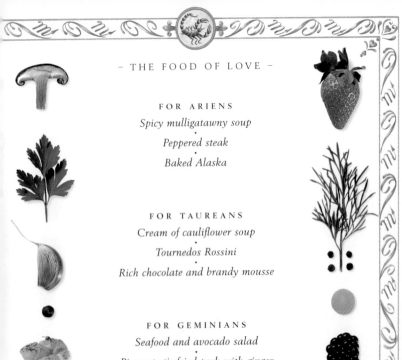

– THE FOOD OF LOVE –

FOR ARIENS
Spicy mulligatawny soup
·
Peppered steak
·
Baked Alaska

FOR TAUREANS
Cream of cauliflower soup
·
Tournedos Rossini
·
Rich chocolate and brandy mousse

FOR GEMINIANS
Seafood and avocado salad
·
Piquant stir-fried pork with ginger
·
Zabaglione

FOR CANCERIANS
Artichoke vinaigrette
·
Sole Bonne Femme
·
Almond soufflé

- THE FOOD OF LOVE -

FOR LEOS
Roasted tomato and garlic soup
·
Boeuf Stroganoff
·
Pears cooked in wine

FOR VIRGOANS
Aubergine salad
·
Paella
·
French apple tart

FOR LIBRANS
Asparagus with hollandaise sauce
·
Pork steak with roasted apples
·
Strawberry Pavlova

FOR SCORPIOS
Vichyssoise
·
Lobster Newburg
·
Blackcurrant fool

- THE FOOD OF LOVE -

FOR SAGITTARIANS
Chilled cucumber soup
·
Nutty onion flan
·
Rhubarb crumble with fresh cream

FOR CAPRICORNIANS
Eggs Florentine
·
Pork tenderloin stuffed with sage
·
Pineapple Pavlova

FOR AQUARIANS
Watercress soup
·
Chicken cooked with chilli and lime
·
Lemon soufflé

FOR PISCEANS
French onion soup
·
Trout au vin rosé
·
Melon sorbet

PLACES TO LOVE

ONCE YOU HAVE WON YOUR LOVER'S HEART, A ROMANTIC
HOLIDAY TOGETHER WILL SET THE SEAL ON YOUR LOVE.
HERE YOU CAN DISCOVER THE PERFECT DESTINATION FOR EACH
SUN SIGN, FROM HISTORIC CITIES TO IDYLLIC BEACHES.

THE
EIFFEL
TOWER,
PARIS

ARIES

*Florence is an Arien
city, and its perfectly
preserved Renaissance
palaces and churches
will set the scene for
wonderful romance.*

TAURUS

*The unspoilt scenery
and unhurried pace
of life in rural Ireland
is sure to appeal to
patient and placid
Taureans.*

GEMINI

*Vivacious and restless
Geminians will feel at
home in the fast-paced
and sophisticated
atmosphere of
New York.*

CANCER

*The watery beauty
and uniquely romantic
atmosphere of Venice
is guaranteed to arouse
passion and stir the
Cancerian imagination.*

ST. BASIL'S
CATHEDRAL,
MOSCOW

AYERS ROCK/ULURU,
AUSTRALIA

LEO

*Leos will fall in love
all over again when
surrounded by the
picturesque charm and
unspoilt medieval
atmosphere of Prague.*

VIRGO

*Perhaps the most
elegant and romantic
of all cities, Paris is
certainly the ideal
setting for a stylish and
fastidious Virgoan.*

LIBRA

*The dramatic and
exotic beauty of Upper
Egypt and the Nile will
provide the perfect
backdrop for wooing
a romantic Libran.*

SCORPIO

*Intense and passionate
Scorpios will be strongly
attracted by the whiff
of danger present in
the exotic atmosphere
of New Orleans.*

SAGITTARIUS

*The wide-ranging
spaces of the Australian
outback will appeal
to the Sagittarian love
of freedom and the
great outdoors.*

CAPRICORN

*Capricornians will be
fascinated and inspired
by the great historical
monuments of Moscow,
the most powerful of all
Russian cities.*

AQUARIUS

*Intrepid Aquarians will
be enthralled and
amazed by the unusual
sights and spectacular
landscapes of the
Indian subcontinent.*

PISCES

*Water-loving Pisceans
will be at their most
relaxed and romantic
by the sea, perhaps on
a small and unspoilt
Mediterranean island.*

THE PYRAMIDS,
EGYPT

GONDOLAS,
VENICE

THE TAJ MAHAL,
INDIA

VENUS & MARS

LUCID, SHINING VENUS AND FIERY, RED MARS HAVE ALWAYS BEEN
ASSOCIATED WITH HUMAN LOVE AND PASSION. THE TWO
PLANETS HAVE A POWERFUL INFLUENCE ON OUR ATTITUDES
TOWARDS LOVE, SEX, AND RELATIONSHIPS.

The study of astrology first began long before humankind began to record its own history. The earliest astrological artefacts discovered, scratches on bones recording the phases of the Moon, date from well before the invention of any alphabet or writing system.

The planets Venus and Mars have always been regarded as having enormous significance in astrology. This is evident from the tentative attempts of early astrologers to record the effects of the two planets on humankind. Hundreds of years later, the positions of the planets were carefully noted in personal horoscopes. The earliest known record is dated 410 BC: "Venus [was] in the Bull, and Mars in the Twins".

The bright, shining planet Venus represents the gentle effect of the soul on our physical lives. It is responsible for a refined and romantic sensuality – "pure" love, untainted by sex. Venus reigns over our attitudes towards romance and the spiritual dimension of love.

The planet Mars affects the physical aspects of our lives – our strength, both physical and mental; our endurance; and our ability to fight for survival. Mars is also strongly linked to the sex drive of both men and women. Mars governs our physical energy, sexuality, and levels of desire.

Venus is known as an "inferior" planet, because its orbit falls between Earth and the Sun. Venus orbits the Sun

LOVE CONQUERS ALL

In Botticelli's Venus and Mars, *the warlike, fiery
energy of Mars, the god of war, has been overcome by
the gentle charms of Venus, the goddess of love.*

closely, and its position in the
zodiac is always in a sign near
that of the Sun. As a result, the
planet can only have occupied
one of five given signs at the
time of your birth – your Sun
sign, or the two signs before or
after it. For example, if you were
born with the Sun in Virgo,
Venus can only have occupied
Cancer, Leo, Virgo, Libra, or
Scorpio at that moment.

Mars, on the other hand, is
a "superior" planet. Its orbit lies
on the other side of the Earth

from the Sun, and therefore the
planet may have occupied any
of the 12 signs at the moment
of your birth.

On the following pages
(24–45) we provide you with
fascinating insights into how
Mars and Venus govern your
attitudes towards love, sex, and
relationships. To ascertain which
sign of the zodiac the planets
occupied at the moment of
your birth, you must first consult
the tables on pages 52–61. Then
turn to page 24 and read on.

YOUR LOVE LIFE

THE PLANET VENUS REPRESENTS LOVE, HARMONY, AND UNISON.
WORK OUT WHICH SIGN OF THE ZODIAC VENUS OCCUPIED AT
THE MOMENT OF YOUR BIRTH (SEE PAGES 52–57), AND READ ON.

VENUS IN VIRGO

*I*ntense, passionate Scorpio appears to have little in common with modest, self-controlled Virgo. However, this placing can prove extremely beneficial, because the self-deprecating and restrained charm of Virgo should be able to temper any Scorpio jealousy.

When Venus shines from Virgo, the sign will not dampen down your Scorpio energy and determination, but it will provide a useful calming influence. Scorpios can find it difficult to express their deep and powerful inner emotions, but from Virgo Venus will bring a talent for communication. Consequently, instead of bottling up your feelings, you should be able to explain to your lover exactly how you feel. The powerful Scorpio sexuality is legendary, and people born under this sign can be swept off their feet by a forceful physical attraction. However, selecting a partner on the basis of a strong sexual attraction does not provide a solid foundation for the growth of a relationship, and can lead to an uneven and unequal alliance. Fortunately, when Venus shines from Virgo, the planet will bring caution and good sense, and you will be less inclined to throw yourself into a relationship.

This planetary placement will make you a generous and compassionate friend. However, Virgo can bring a critical side to your personality, and there is a danger that the energy of

Scorpio could lead you to carp and complain in a harsh and ill-natured manner. Try to express any criticisms in a constructive and tactful fashion.

Both Scorpios and Virgoans tend to be perfectionists. You are likely to be a hard taskmaster, and can judge yourself and others by unrealistically high standards. If you demand too much of yourself, you may be setting yourself up to fail.

Due to the modesty of Virgo, you may underestimate your powers of attraction, and may even be timid when it comes to approaching a potential lover. However, you should not lack self-confidence, for the shy charm of Virgo is highly attractive. If you can combine Scorpio passion and intensity with Virgoan charm and modesty, you are guaranteed to enjoy great success when it comes to romance.

VENUS IN LIBRA

*T*his planetary placing will have a very positive effect on Sun-sign Scorpios. It will bring a tender and romantic air to the intense energy and potent sexuality of Scorpio, and as a result, you will be a loving and considerate partner.

When Venus shines from Libra, you will be motivated by a fundamental desire to form a stable relationship and settle down in domestic harmony. This eagerness to form a permanent alliance, along with your Scorpio intensity and passion, may persuade you to throw yourself recklessly into new relationships. However, before becoming involved with someone, you must pause for a moment and reflect on how well suited you are to your potential lover. Even you, with your abundance of Scorpio energy, will not be able to salvage an ill-matched and unbalanced relationship.

The formidable strength and determination of Scorpio can make those born under this Sun sign appear rather abrasive and aggressive. However, when Venus occupies Libra, a welcome dose of tact and diplomacy will soften these qualities. Your sympathy and understanding should win you a wide circle of friends, and you will always be ready to provide them with support, consolation, and encouragement. You are extremely loyal, and once the bonds of friendship have been formed, it will take a great deal to sever them.

Scorpio love affairs can be stormy. If people born under this sign are not fulfilled and satisfied by their emotional relationships, the energy and passion of the sign might be channelled into jealousy and broodiness. Scorpios have a tendency to suppress all their worries and problems, rather than addressing them in

a rational and realistic fashion. Jealousy and suspicion may build up unchecked, culminating in a violent explosion of resentment. Fortunately, jealousy should not present too much of a problem for Scorpios born with Venus in Libra. Due to this position of Venus you are likely to be easy-going and even-tempered, and your innate fairness should counter any tendency towards irrational jealousy.

Libra is the sign of the scales, and anyone born with Venus in this sign will strive to attain balance and harmony in all their emotional relationships. This planetary placing will have a most beneficial effect on the Scorpio personality, because the fundamental dynamism, passion, and intensity of the sign will be tempered, but not suppressed, by the peaceful, loving, and romantic influence of Libra.

VENUS IN SCORPIO

*W*hen both Venus and the Sun are placed in Scorpio, all your typical Scorpio traits will be accentuated, and your ardent and passionate attitude to love and emotional relationships will prove quite irresistible to potential lovers.

Many Scorpios are driven by the need to form a harmonious and secure permanent alliance. Once attracted by a potential partner, you will channel all your formidable Scorpio energy into pursuing the object of your affections, even if it is obvious that he or she is totally unsuited to you. You must choose a lover wisely, or your relationship will be doomed to failure.

Scorpios are renowned for their vigorous sexuality, therefore the physical side of your affair must be exciting and rewarding. If you do not enjoy an active and regular sex life, you may become frustrated and dissatisfied.

Once you have found a partner you are happy with, you will be an adoring lover. However, do not allow your passion to get out of hand. You will put great effort into a love affair, but try not to become too obsessive about your relationship. Your intensity may alarm your lover, and there is a danger that you may unwittingly create a claustrophobic atmosphere. Try to understand that most people want to retain a degree of freedom within their long-term relationship.

The Scorpio tendency towards jealousy may be exacerbated by this placing of Venus. Try to quash this emotion as soon as it rears its ugly head, because it will only make you possessive and suspicious. You must not bottle up any worries and fears about your relationship, because once you become overwrought you are difficult to reason with.

Instead, voice your doubts to your partner – he or she should soon be able to allay any unjustified suspicions.

Scorpios are usually loyal and constant friends as well as lovers. Once you have pledged your love and support, it will not be lightly withdrawn. However, you can be over-sensitive, and when you feel that a friend has let you down, you may ruthlessly sever all ties with them.

You possess an abundance of love and passion which, if used positively, will help you to form a long-lasting, emotionally and sexually fulfilling relationship, and to forge bonds that are not easily broken. Do not allow your intensity to dominate your relationships. If you can adopt a more light-hearted and relaxed attitude to life, you will prove to be an extremely captivating and beguiling lover.

VENUS IN SAGITTARIUS

*W*hen Venus shines from Sagittarius, the bright and breezy influence of the sign will lighten the intensity of the Scorpio attitude to love. This planetary placing will bring you plenty of common sense and a philosphical attitude to life. You will possess an abundance of Scorpio passion, yet will express your feelings with the honesty and directness of Sagittarius.

Your strong Scorpio sexuality will not be dampened by this placing. Your enthusiasm for love and sex will be evident, and you will have no shortage of admirers. However, due to this position of Venus, an intellectual rapport with your lover will be just as important to you as an active and vigorous sex life.

The influence of Venus from Sagittarius will encourage a restless streak in your personality, and you will constantly seek excitement and novelty.

You need a lively and eventful relationship – any hint of monotony will soon sound the death knell for your alliance. Sagittarians are the hunters of the zodiac, and they thrive on the challenge of the chase, often losing interest once they have won the heart of a potential partner. You may operate on the principle that there is always something better around the next corner, but you must learn to make the most of what you have rather than constantly searching for something new.

Sagittarian duality will be evident in your personality, and you may be tempted by illicit liaisons. Scorpios tend to be extremely faithful partners, and infidelity is not something you will undertake lightly. You may become caught in a web of guilt and confusion, therefore try to resist the temptation to become involved in clandestine affairs.

This planetary placing will bring you a love of freedom which should counteract any Scorpio jealousy. You need your independence, and cannot bear to feel restricted. However, if your lover demands a measure of freedom, the powerful influence of Scorpio is likely to reassert itself, and you may experience some painful pangs of jealousy. You cannot expect your partner to live by one set of rules while you abide by another, therefore enlist the help of philosophical Sagittarius to help you control any possessiveness or jealousy.

When Venus shines from Sagittarius, the optimism and cheerfulness of the sign will alleviate your Scorpio intensity. You will remain a passionate lover, yet the openness and honesty of Sagittarius should easily overcome any Scorpio jealousy and secretiveness.

VENUS IN CAPRICORN

*T*his placing will combine the deep intensity and passion of Scorpio with the cool calculation of Capricorn. Your forcefulness and determination will not be lessened, but your passionate Scorpio emotions will be checked by the practical, disciplined influence of Venus in Capricorn. A formal and distant exterior can be extremely intriguing and tantalizing, and you may find that your remote and aloof air wins you a multitude of admirers.

When Venus shines from Capricorn, the determination and obstinacy of Scorpio will be doubled, and you are likely to be utterly ruthless when it comes to getting your own way. You will also be extremely persistent when pursuing a potential lover. Anyone you set your sights on will soon be bowled over by your magnetic personality and forceful attentions.

When Scorpios meet someone they are attracted to, they tend to fall heavily and deeply in love, without holding back, and express their feelings with ardour and passion. However, with Venus in Capricorn, you will be extremely cautious about making a long-term commitment. You are of a practical turn of mind, and will not want to invest your powerful Scorpio emotions in a love affair unless you are convinced that your potential partner is perfectly suited to you. As a result, you are likely to give much consideration to choosing a lover.

However, there is a danger that Venus, from this sign, could encourage you to choose a lover for all the wrong reasons – simply because they are good-looking, wealthy, or influential, and therefore likely to impress your friends and aquaintances. Selecting a partner on such

superficial grounds will not lead to a happy, well-balanced, and long-lasting relationship.

Once committed, you will be a faithful and loving partner, and the thought of infidelity will not appeal. You may be embarrassed by overt displays of emotion, preferring to retain a dignified facade, but you must try to express your true feelings. Do not conceal your powerful Scorpio emotions too well.

When Venus occupies Capricorn, you will be a very motivated, determined, and self-controlled partner. The cool and practical influence of the sign will calm your tempestuous Scorpio emotions, and enable you to approach your relationships in a more considered and balanced fashion. However, your intense and powerful Scorpio passion will always prove seductive and beguiling to potential partners.

YOUR SEX LIFE

THE PLANET MARS REPRESENTS PHYSICAL AND SEXUAL ENERGY.
WORK OUT WHICH SIGN OF THE ZODIAC MARS OCCUPIED AT THE
MOMENT OF YOUR BIRTH (SEE PAGES 58–61), AND READ ON.

MARS IN ARIES

The vigorous energy, forcefulness, and overt sexuality of Mars in Aries will enhance your powerful Scorpio emotions. This placing will make you a passionate, spirited lover, with plenty of stamina and vigour.

You must find a partner who shares your prodigious appetite for sex, because if you are not able to satisfy your powerful sex drive, you may become restless and dissatisfied.

The forthright influence of Mars in Aries will make your intense Scorpio sexuality more open and spontaneous. As a result, your lovemaking will be passionate and dynamic, yet honest and uncomplicated.

MARS IN TAURUS

*F*rom Taurus, Mars will maintain your powerful Scorpio sex drive, but the planet will add a sensual and affectionate element to your lovemaking. You will be a passionate lover, and your ardour and tenderness will thrill and delight your partner.

Taurean warmth will soothe the cold and resentful anger of Scorpio, and you will have to be sorely provoked before you lose your temper. However, once your anger is roused, your feelings will flood out in force.

Try to remember that outbursts of rage may relieve your feelings, but there is a danger that they may also intimidate your lover.

Scorpios can suffer from sexual jealousy, and when Mars shines from Taurus, you may be prone to possessiveness – a very dangerous combination. Do not allow a stifling atmosphere to pervade your relationship. Instead, channel your formidable energies into a fulfilling sex life, and reap the benefits of your partner's delight.

MARS IN GEMINI

With this placing, you may display a tendency to plunge into love affairs even more swiftly and passionately than the majority of your fellow Scorpios. You will expect your sexual relationships to develop quickly, and will be a seductive and imaginative lover.

The lively and flirtatious influence of Mars in Gemini will lighten your Scorpio intensity and fervour. You will adopt a far more light-hearted and carefree attitude towards your relationships, and any deep-seated Scorpio tendency towards jealousy will be lessened.

Scorpios are usually faithful partners, but when Mars occupies Gemini, the planet tends to be in a restless mood. Intrigue and infidelity will appeal to you, and you could even become involved in several affairs at the same time, causing terrible complications. You should not need infidelity to give you a thrill, because your sex life is likely to be adventurous and fulfilling.

– YOUR SEX LIFE –

MARS IN CANCER

*T*he watery and volatile emotions of Cancer will combine with the physical passion of Scorpio to make you an extremely sensual, protective, and tender lover. You will be instinctively aware of your partner's needs and desires, and will be eager to satisfy them.

You will be an extremely caring and demonstrative partner, but must make sure that you do not become over-protective and clinging. There is a slight danger that you may create a confining and claustrophobic atmosphere within your relationship. Do not become too intense – your lover may be alarmed by the depth of your emotions. Stop worrying, and try to become a little more rational and practical.

The high emotion of Scorpio, combined with the sensitivity of Cancer, may lead to sudden oubursts of rage, largely fuelled by wounded feelings. In moments of anger, you can be very hurtful, therefore make an effort to guard your scathing tongue.

MARS IN LEO

*F*rom Leo, Mars will bring many beneficial characteristics to a Sun-sign Scorpio. The optimistic, forthright influence of Mars in Leo will lighten the energy and passion of Scorpio, and you will be a warm-hearted and exuberant lover, with a multitude of admirers.

You will revel in your uncomplicated sexuality, and will expect your lover to share your enjoyment of sex. Your love-making will be enthusiastic and rewarding, and is likely to take place in the most luxurious of surroundings. The influence of Leo may encourage you to be a little domineering and dictatorial. You must resist the temptation to take control and start telling your lover what to do and how to run his or her life.

You secretly relish scenes and dramas, but try not to become too much of an exhibitionist. With this placing, you may have a quick and fiery temper, but luckily you will swiftly forget any altercations or tantrums.

MARS IN VIRGO

The calm, self-contained influence of Virgo will prove invaluable when it comes to taming powerful Scorpio emotions. You will still be a passionate and energetic lover, but due to the influence of Virgo you will be more down-to-earth and practical than many Scorpios and will not be prey to such intense and extreme emotions.

Scorpio can be a secretive and enigmatic sign, but Virgo is ruled by Mercury, the planet of communication, therefore the influence of Virgo will make you more open and honest. You are less likely to bottle up your worries and fears, and will find it easier to explain your feelings and give voice to your emotions.

Virgo is a practical and sensible sign, and with this placing you will not suffer the painful jealousy experienced by so many Scorpios. You will fight off any groundless suspicions with ease, and as a result, your relationship will possess an open, honest, and loving atmosphere.

MARS IN LIBRA

The languid, sensual, and relaxing influence of Mars in Libra will lessen the power and intensity of Scorpio sexuality. You may even possess a rather lethargic attitude to sex, and might sometimes try to avoid it altogether. Remember there is a limit to the number of headaches you can feign in one week.

However, once you are aroused your partner will have no complaints, because your sensuality will be heightened by this placing of the planet.

When you throw off the rather torpid influence of Libra, you will make love passionately, enthusiastically, and skilfully.

From Libra, the gentle influence of Mars will bring you a strong streak of romance. If you manage to combine the softness and sensuality that is characteristic of Mars in Libra with the passion and dynamic sexuality so typical of Scorpio, you should be a powerfully attractive lover with a multitude of potential partners.

MARS IN SCORPIO

*W*hen both Mars and the Sun find themselves in the same sign, your sexual vigour is greatly emphasized. You will be an intensely passionate and erotic lover, with a powerful sex drive and plenty of stamina.

You are likely to possess an abundance of sexual energy, and must find a fulfilling outlet for your passions. In order to form a satisfying relationship that will stand the test of time, you must find a partner who possesses an equally strong sexual appetite.

There is wonderful potential in this dynamic combination, but there is a danger that the Scorpio tendency towards jealousy may cause you a few problems. You will have to devise a strategy for dealing with possessiveness and jealousy, because these emotions could damage your relationship beyond repair. You must accept your tendency to be unreasonably jealous, and teach yourself to dispel your suspicions by adopting a rational and sensible approach.

MARS IN SAGITTARIUS

*T*his planetary placing will give an enormous boost to your physical energy, and you will be an adventurous, dynamic, and passionate lover.

Scorpios tend to be extremely loyal and constant partners, but the influence of Sagittarius may tempt you to become involved in illicit affairs and to be unfaithful to your lover. There is an element of duality present in Sagittarius which will enable you to savour the thrill of infidelity and intrigue. You tend to be restless and easily bored, but do not give up a happy relationship just because you think that there may be something more exciting on the horizon. The benefits of stability and security should never be underestimated.

Sagittarius is an intensely independent and self-sufficient sign, therefore this planetary placing will help to combat any Scorpio jealousy. You treasure your independence and will allow your lovers a measure of freedom.

MARS IN CAPRICORN

Scorpios born with Mars in Capricorn will be ambitious and highly motivated, and all your formidable Scorpio energies will be concentrated on winning the heart of a potential partner. Once committed, you will be a forceful and passionate lover with plenty of stamina.

The coolness and restraint of Capricorn will tone down your tempestuous Scorpio emotions, and you will be more self-controlled and disciplined than many of your fellow Scorpios.

This placing will enable you to channel your remarkable energies into your career as well as your sex drive, and you are likely to be an extremely successful high achiever. However, do not put so much of your energy into your work that you neglect your lover.

When the practicality and determination of Capricorn is combined with the ardour and passion of Scorpio, you will be a seductive and forceful lover, and will swiftly seduce anyone you set your sights on.

MARS IN AQUARIUS

*W*hen Mars shines from Aquarius, the planet will soften the urgency and fervour of your emotional and physical expression of love. Although the cool and introverted influence of Aquarius may lessen the intensity of your Scorpio emotions, you will still be a passionate and adventurous lover.

Aquarius is an unconventional and idiosyncratic sign, and your individuality and unpredictability is guaranteed to delight your partner. You will enjoy sex and will be eager to experiment, although the detachment and restraint so typical of Aquarius may slightly weaken your highly-charged Scorpio sex drive.

Scorpios are usually at their happiest within a secure long-term relationship, but you may find the prospect of giving up your independence and settling down unappealing. Aquarius is a free-spirited sign, therefore the prospect of permanent involvement might make you feel a little claustrophobic.

MARS IN PISCES

The ardent and sensual influence of Mars in Pisces will raise your already high emotional temperature, and because Scorpios are renowned for their passion, intensity, and high sex drive, no lover of yours is likely to complain of neglect.

If your sexual and emotional energy is not rewardingly and imaginatively directed, you may grow dissatisfied and frustrated. However, this does not mean that you should select a lover solely on the grounds of sexual attraction. Sex should not be the central focus of your alliance – several mutual interests and a stimulating intellectual rapport are also essential ingredients for a successful and long-lasting emotional relationship.

Scorpios revel in mystery and secrecy, and this planetary placing may also bring a tendency towards evasiveness and concealment. Resist the temptation to bottle up your feelings, and strive to be entirely open and honest with your lover.

TOKENS OF LOVE

ASTROLOGY CAN GIVE YOU A FASCINATING INSIGHT INTO
YOUR LOVER'S PERSONALITY AND ATTITUDE TO LOVE. IT CAN
ALSO PROVIDE YOU WITH SOME INVALUABLE HINTS WHEN YOU
WANT TO CHOOSE THE PERFECT GIFT FOR YOUR LOVER.

ARIES
*Sports equipment is
certain to please active
Ariens. Aromatherapy
massage oils will also
delight a sensual Arien lover. The
head is the part of the body ruled
by Aries, and unusual hair products
and accessories will be appreciated.*

SHUTTLECOCKS

MASSAGE
OILS

CHOCOLATE
CAKE

JEWELLED HAIR
SLIDE

TAURUS
*Taureans value quality
above quantity. A rich
chocolate cake or
Belgian chocolates
will appeal to
the Taurean
sweet tooth.*

GEMINI
*A handsome box
of exotic nuts is
guaranteed to
delight your
Geminian
lover.*

CRYSTALLIZED
CHESTNUTS

– TOKENS OF LOVE –

CANCER

Objects with a moon motif will delight a Cancerian. A sunshade makes an ideal gift, because Cancerians take good care of their skin.

ENAMELLED
PILLBOX

SUNFLOWER
PEN

GOLD
'COCKTAIL'
WRISTWATCH

LEO

Gold is the Leo metal, and anything made from this metal is sure to please. Sunflower motifs will also be popular with Leos.

PAINTED
CHINESE
SUNSHADE

VIRGO

Virgo, an earth sign, naturally loves gardening. Potted plants or garden implements will be gratefully received.

ANGEL WINGS
POTTED PLANT

1930s'
LUDO
BOARD

WHITE
ROSES

LIBRA

*Board or card games will
suit a Libran lover. Librans
are true romantics and will
be enraptured by a
bouquet of white roses.*

SCORPIO

*Scorpios will be
delighted by a
handsome leather
wallet. A cocktail
shaker would also
be an ideal gift.*

LEATHER
WALLET

19TH-
CENTURY
ENGRAVING
OF A HOT-
AIR BALLOON

SAGITTARIUS

*Your Sagittarian
lover will be thrilled
by the gift of an
unusual experience,
such as a flight in
a hot-air balloon.*

ART DECO
COCKTAIL
SHAKER

SILVER
PICTURE
FRAME

GIVING A BIRTHSTONE

*The most personal
gift you can give
your lover is the
gem linked to his
or her Sun sign.*

OPAL

ARIES: *diamond*
TAURUS: *emerald*
GEMINI: *agate* • CANCER: *pearl*
LEO: *ruby* • VIRGO: *sardonyx*
LIBRA: *sapphire* • SCORPIO: *opal*
SAGITTARIUS: *topaz*
CAPRICORN: *amethyst*
AQUARIUS: *aquamarine*
PISCES: *moonstone*

CAPRICORN

BUTTERFLY
BROOCH

*A silver picture
frame or fine
fountain pen
will impress
a fastidious
Capricornian
lover.*

AQUARIUS

DECORATIVE
SHELL

ORCHIDS

*Glittery pieces of
costume jewellery
will charm an
Aquarian. If you
want to give an
Aquarian flowers,
choose orchids.*

PISCES

*Pisces is a water sign,
and Pisceans love the
sea, therefore a decorative
shell or piece of mother-of-
pearl is guaranteed to please.*

YOUR PERMANENT RELATIONSHIP

SCORPIOS ARE INTENSE AND PASSIONATE LOVERS, HAPPY TO
DEVOTE MUCH ENERGY TO THEIR PERMANENT RELATIONSHIPS.
HOWEVER, SCORPIO JEALOUSY MUST BE CAREFULLY CONTROLLED.

Scorpios may find it hard to modify their behaviour when they commit themselves to a long-term relationship – and their natural stubbornness will not help them to adapt.

Scorpios are not known for half measures, and you will expect at least as much out of your relationship as you put into it. Despite your notorious preoccupation with sex, in reality your sex life and emotional involvement must be evenly balanced. You need a partner who is as eager as you are to make things work, and who has similar levels of emotional and physical energy.

Sexuality is not the only driving force in a Scorpio's life.

Your enormous resources of energy need constant and positive expression if you are to be happy and fulfilled. Scorpios tend to be very ambitious, and you will work hard to achieve a high standard of living.

Ideally, your partner will share your sense of drive and motivation, and if this is the case, you should have little difficulty in jointly attaining your ambitions. However, your determination to succeed may cause you to neglect your partner and family. Set aside time for your domestic life, and make sure your children do not suffer from lack of attention.

Most Scorpios are diligent and industrious, but the dangers of overwork are overshadowed by the dangers of too much

A JOINT FUTURE

On a Sailing Ship, by Caspar David Friedrich, shows a newly-married couple sailing into a bright but unknown future together.

enforced leisure. When Scorpios are unfulfilled, the most negative characteristics of the sign reveal themselves – suspicion, resentment, and jealousy. Your partner may not comprehend the strength of your ambitions, or your frustration when you cannot achieve them. Try to solve any problems by discussing them openly and honestly with your lover.

You may become irrationally jealous and suspicious if your partner devotes too much time to work or other friends. Jealousy is an emotion to which Scorpios are naturally disposed, and it can destroy a happy relationship. A shared interest will ensure that you spend a great deal of your time together working towards a common goal. This will make you less likely to succumb to unreasonable jealousy.

VENUS & MARS TABLES

THESE TABLES WILL ENABLE YOU TO DISCOVER WHICH SIGNS
VENUS AND MARS OCCUPIED AT THE MOMENT OF YOUR BIRTH.
TURN TO PAGES 24–45 TO INVESTIGATE THE QUALITIES OF THESE
SIGNS, AND TO FIND OUT HOW THEY WORK WITH YOUR SUN SIGN.

*T*he tables on pages 53–61 will enable you to discover the positions of Venus and Mars at the moment of your birth.

First find your year of birth on the top line of the appropriate table, then find your month of birth in the left-hand column. Where the column for your year of birth intersects with the row for your month of birth, you will find a group of figures and zodiacal glyphs. These figures and glyphs show which sign of the zodiac the planet occupied

on the first day of that month, and any date during that month on which the planet moved into another sign.

For example, to ascertain the position of Venus on May 10 1968, run your finger down the column marked 1968 until you reach the row for May. The row of numbers and glyphs shows that Venus occupied Aries on May 1, entered Taurus on May 4, and then moved into Gemini on May 28. Therefore, on May 10, Venus was in Taurus.

If you were born on a day when one of the planets was moving into a new sign, it may be impossible to determine your Venus and Mars signs completely accurately. If the characteristics described on the relevant pages do not seem to apply to you, read the interpretation of the sign before and after. One of these signs will be appropriate.

ZODIACAL GLYPHS

♈	Aries	♎	Libra
♉	Taurus	♏	Scorpio
♊	Gemini	♐	Sagittarius
♋	Cancer	♑	Capricorn
♌	Leo	♒	Aquarius
♍	Virgo	♓	Pisces

– VENUS TABLES –

♀	1921	1922	1923	1924	1925	1926	1927	1928
JAN	1 ♒ · 7 ♓	1 ♑ · 25 ♒	1 ♏ · 3 ♐	1 ♒ · 20 ♓	1 ♐ · 15 ♑	1 ♒	1 ♑ · 10 ♒	1 ♏ · 5 ♐ · 30 ♑
FEB	1 ♓ · 3 ♈	1 ♒ · 18 ♓	1 ♐ · 7 ♑	1 ♓ · 14 ♈	1 ♑ · 8 ♒	1 ♒	1 ♒ · 3 ♓ · 27 ♈	1 ♑ · 23 ♒
MAR	1 ♈ · 8 ♉	1 ♓ · 14 ♈	1 ♑ · 7 ♒	1 ♈ · 10 ♉	1 ♒ · 5 ♓ · 29 ♈	1 ♒	1 ♈ · 23 ♉	1 ♒ · 19 ♓
APR	1 ♉ · 26 ♈	1 ♈ · 7 ♉	1 ♒ · 2 ♓ · 27 ♈	1 ♉ · 6 ♊	1 ♈ · 22 ♉	1 ♒ · 7 ♓	1 ♉ · 17 ♊	1 ♓ · 12 ♈
MAY	1 ♈	1 ♉ · 2 ♊ · 26 ♋	1 ♈ · 22 ♉	1 ♊ · 7 ♋	1 ♉ · 16 ♊	1 ♓ · 7 ♈	1 ♊ · 13 ♋	1 ♈ · 7 ♉ · 31 ♊
JUN	1 ♈ · 8 ♉	1 ♋ · 20 ♌	1 ♉ · 16 ♊	1 ♋	1 ♊ · 10 ♋	1 ♈ · 3 ♉ · 29 ♊	1 ♋ · 9 ♌	1 ♊ · 24 ♋
JUL	1 ♉ · 9 ♊	1 ♌ · 16 ♍	1 ♊ · 11 ♋	1 ♋	1 ♋ · 4 ♌ · 29 ♍	1 ♊ · 25 ♋	1 ♌ · 8 ♍	1 ♋ · 19 ♌
AUG	1 ♊ · 6 ♋	1 ♍ · 11 ♎	1 ♋ · 4 ♌ · 28 ♍	1 ♋	1 ♍ · 23 ♎	1 ♋ · 19 ♌	1 ♍	1 ♌ · 12 ♍
SEP	1 ♌ · 27 ♍	1 ♎ · 8 ♏	1 ♍ · 22 ♎	1 ♋ · 8 ♌	1 ♎ · 17 ♏	1 ♌ · 12 ♍	1 ♍	1 ♍ · 5 ♎ · 30 ♏
OCT	1 ♍ · 21 ♎	1 ♏ · 11 ♐	1 ♎ · 16 ♏	1 ♌ · 8 ♍	1 ♏ · 12 ♐	1 ♍ · 6 ♎ · 30 ♏	1 ♍	1 ♏ · 24 ♐
NOV	1 ♎ · 14 ♏	1 ♐ · 29 ♏	1 ♏ · 9 ♐	1 ♍ · 3 ♎ · 28 ♏	1 ♐ · 7 ♑	1 ♏ · 23 ♐	1 ♍ · 10 ♎	1 ♐ · 18 ♑
DEC	1 ♏ · 8 ♐ · 31 ♑	1 ♏	1 ♐ · 3 ♑ · 27 ♒	1 ♏ · 22 ♐	1 ♑ · 6 ♒	1 ♐ · 17 ♑	1 ♎ · 9 ♏	1 ♑ · 13 ♒

♀	1929	1930	1931	1932	1933	1934	1935	1936
JAN	1 ♒ · 7 ♓	1 ♑ · 25 ♒	1 ♏ · 4 ♐	1 ♒ · 20 ♓	1 ♐ · 15 ♑	1 ♒	1 ♑ · 9 ♒	1 ♏ · 4 ♐ · 29 ♑
FEB	1 ♓ · 3 ♈	1 ♒ · 17 ♓	1 ♐ · 7 ♑	1 ♓ · 13 ♈	1 ♑ · 8 ♒	1 ♒	1 ♒ · 2 ♓ · 27 ♈	1 ♑ · 23 ♒
MAR	1 ♈ · 9 ♉	1 ♓ · 13 ♈	1 ♑ · 6 ♒	1 ♈ · 10 ♉	1 ♒ · 4 ♓ · 28 ♈	1 ♒	1 ♈ · 23 ♉	1 ♒ · 18 ♓
APR	1 ♉ · 21 ♈	1 ♈ · 7 ♉	1 ♒ · 2 ♓ · 27 ♈	1 ♉ · 6 ♊	1 ♈ · 21 ♉	1 ♒ · 7 ♓	1 ♉ · 17 ♊	1 ♓ · 12 ♈
MAY	1 ♈	1 ♊ · 26 ♋	1 ♈ · 22 ♉	1 ♊ · 7 ♋	1 ♉ · 16 ♊	1 ♓ · 7 ♈	1 ♊ · 12 ♋	1 ♈ · 6 ♉ · 30 ♊
JUN	1 ♈ · 4 ♉	1 ♋ · 20 ♌	1 ♉ · 15 ♊	1 ♋	1 ♊ · 9 ♋	1 ♈ · 3 ♉ · 29 ♊	1 ♋ · 8 ♌	1 ♊ · 24 ♋
JUL	1 ♉ · 9 ♊	1 ♌ · 15 ♍	1 ♊ · 10 ♋	1 ♋ · 14 ♊ · 29 ♋	1 ♋ · 4 ♌ · 28 ♍	1 ♊ · 24 ♋	1 ♌ · 8 ♍	1 ♋ · 18 ♌
AUG	1 ♊ · 6 ♋	1 ♍ · 11 ♎	1 ♋ · 4 ♌ · 28 ♍	1 ♋	1 ♍ · 22 ♎	1 ♋ · 18 ♌	1 ♍	1 ♌ · 12 ♍
SEP	1 ♌ · 26 ♍	1 ♎ · 8 ♏	1 ♍ · 21 ♎	1 ♋ · 9 ♌	1 ♎ · 16 ♏	1 ♌ · 12 ♍	1 ♍	1 ♍ · 5 ♎ · 29 ♏
OCT	1 ♍ · 21 ♎	1 ♏ · 13 ♐	1 ♎ · 15 ♏	1 ♌ · 9 ♍	1 ♏ · 12 ♐	1 ♍ · 6 ♎ · 30 ♏	1 ♍	1 ♏ · 24 ♐
NOV	1 ♎ · 14 ♏	1 ♐ · 23 ♏	1 ♏ · 8 ♐	1 ♍ · 2 ♎ · 28 ♏	1 ♐ · 7 ♑	1 ♏ · 23 ♐	1 ♍ · 10 ♎	1 ♐ · 17 ♑
DEC	1 ♏ · 8 ♐ · 31 ♑	1 ♏	1 ♐ · 2 ♑ · 26 ♒	1 ♏ · 22 ♐	1 ♑ · 6 ♒	1 ♐ · 17 ♑	1 ♎ · 9 ♏	1 ♑ · 12 ♒

– VENUS TABLES –

♀	1937	1938	1939	1940	1941	1942	1943	1944
JAN	1 ♒, 7 ♓	1 ♑, 24 ♒	1 ♏, 5 ♐	1 ♒, 19 ♓	1 ♐, 14 ♑	1 ♒	1 ♑, 9 ♒	1 ♏, 4 ♐, 29 ♑
FEB	1 ♓, 3 ♈	1 ♒, 17 ♓	1 ♐, 7 ♑	1 ♓, 13 ♈	1 ♑, 7 ♒	1 ♒	1 ♒, 2 ♓, 26 ♈	1 ♑, 22 ♒
MAR	1 ♈, 10 ♉	1 ♓, 13 ♈	1 ♑, 6 ♒, 29 ♓	1 ♈, 9 ♉	1 ♒, 3 ♓, 28 ♈	1 ♒	1 ♈, 22 ♉	1 ♒, 18 ♓
APR	1 ♉, 15 ♈	1 ♈, 6 ♉, 30 ♊	1 ♓, 26 ♈	1 ♉, 5 ♊	1 ♈, 21 ♉	1 ♒, 7 ♓	1 ♉, 16 ♊	1 ♓, 11 ♈
MAY	1 ♈	1 ♊, 25 ♋	1 ♈, 21 ♉	1 ♊, 7 ♋	1 ♉, 15 ♊	1 ♓, 7 ♈	1 ♊, 12 ♋	1 ♈, 5 ♉, 30 ♊
JUN	1 ♈, 5 ♉	1 ♋, 19 ♌	1 ♉, 15 ♊	1 ♋, 28 ♊	1 ♊, 8 ♋	1 ♈, 3 ♉, 28 ♊	1 ♋, 8 ♌	1 ♊, 23 ♋
JUL	1 ♉, 8 ♊	1 ♌, 15 ♍	1 ♊, 10 ♋	1 ♊	1 ♋, 3 ♌, 28 ♍	1 ♊, 24 ♋	1 ♌, 8 ♍	1 ♋, 18 ♌
AUG	1 ♊, 5 ♋, 29 ♌	1 ♍, 10 ♎	1 ♋, 3 ♌, 27 ♍	1 ♊, 2 ♋	1 ♍, 22 ♎	1 ♋, 18 ♌	1 ♍	1 ♌, 11 ♍
SEP	1 ♌, 26 ♍	1 ♎, 8 ♏	1 ♍, 21 ♎	1 ♋, 9 ♌	1 ♎, 16 ♏	1 ♌, 11 ♍	1 ♍	1 ♍, 4 ♎, 29 ♏
OCT	1 ♍, 20 ♎	1 ♏, 14 ♐	1 ♎, 15 ♏	1 ♌, 7 ♍	1 ♏, 11 ♐	1 ♍, 5 ♎, 29 ♏	1 ♍	1 ♏, 23 ♐
NOV	1 ♎, 13 ♏	1 ♐, 16 ♏	1 ♏, 8 ♐	1 ♍, 2 ♎, 27 ♏	1 ♐, 7 ♑	1 ♏, 22 ♐	1 ♍, 10 ♎	1 ♐, 17 ♑
DEC	1 ♏, 7 ♐, 31 ♑	1 ♏	1 ♐, 2 ♑, 26 ♒	1 ♏, 21 ♐	1 ♑, 6 ♒	1 ♐, 16 ♑	1 ♎, 9 ♏	1 ♑, 12 ♒

♀	1945	1946	1947	1948	1949	1950	1951	1952
JAN	1 ♒, 6 ♓	1 ♑, 23 ♒	1 ♏, 6 ♐	1 ♒, 19 ♓	1 ♐, 14 ♑	1 ♒	1 ♑, 8 ♒	1 ♏, 3 ♐, 28 ♑
FEB	1 ♓, 3 ♈	1 ♒, 16 ♓	1 ♐, 7 ♑	1 ♓, 12 ♈	1 ♑, 7 ♒	1 ♒	1 ♓, 25 ♈	1 ♑, 21 ♒
MAR	1 ♈, 12 ♉	1 ♓, 12 ♈	1 ♑, 6 ♒, 31 ♓	1 ♈, 9 ♉	1 ♒, 3 ♓, 27 ♈	1 ♒	1 ♈, 22 ♉	1 ♒, 17 ♓
APR	1 ♉, 8 ♈	1 ♈, 6 ♉, 30 ♊	1 ♓, 26 ♈	1 ♉, 5 ♊	1 ♈, 20 ♉	1 ♒, 7 ♓	1 ♉, 16 ♊	1 ♓, 10 ♈
MAY	1 ♈	1 ♊, 25 ♋	1 ♈, 21 ♉	1 ♊, 8 ♋	1 ♉, 15 ♊	1 ♓, 6 ♈	1 ♊, 12 ♋	1 ♈, 5 ♉, 29 ♊
JUN	1 ♈, 19 ♉	1 ♋, 19 ♌	1 ♉, 14 ♊	1 ♋, 30 ♊	1 ♊, 8 ♋	1 ♈, 2 ♉, 28 ♊	1 ♋, 8 ♌	1 ♊, 23 ♋
JUL	1 ♉, 14 ♊	1 ♌, 14 ♍	1 ♊, 9 ♋	1 ♊	1 ♋, 2 ♌, 27 ♍	1 ♊, 23 ♋	1 ♌, 9 ♍	1 ♋, 17 ♌
AUG	1 ♊, 5 ♋, 31 ♌	1 ♍, 10 ♎	1 ♋, 3 ♌, 27 ♍	1 ♊, 4 ♋	1 ♍, 21 ♎	1 ♋, 17 ♌	1 ♍	1 ♌, 10 ♍
SEP	1 ♌, 25 ♍	1 ♎, 8 ♏	1 ♍, 20 ♎	1 ♋, 9 ♌	1 ♎, 15 ♏	1 ♌, 11 ♍	1 ♍	1 ♍, 4 ♎, 28 ♏
OCT	1 ♍, 17 ♎	1 ♏, 17 ♐	1 ♎, 14 ♏	1 ♌, 9 ♍	1 ♏, 11 ♐	1 ♍, 5 ♎, 29 ♏	1 ♍	1 ♏, 23 ♐
NOV	1 ♎, 13 ♏	1 ♐, 9 ♏	1 ♏, 7 ♐	1 ♍, 2 ♎, 27 ♏	1 ♐, 7 ♑	1 ♏, 22 ♐	1 ♍, 10 ♎	1 ♐, 16 ♑
DEC	1 ♏, 7 ♐, 31 ♑	1 ♏	1 ♑, 24 ♒	1 ♏, 21 ♐	1 ♑, 7 ♒	1 ♐, 15 ♑	1 ♎, 9 ♏	1 ♑, 11 ♒

♀	1953	1954	1955	1956	1957	1958	1959	1960
JAN	1 ♒ 6 ♓	1 ♑ 23 ♒	1 ♏ 7 ♐	1 ♒ 18 ♓	1 ♐ 13 ♑	1 ♒	1 ♑ 8 ♒	1 ♏ 3 ♐ 28 ♑
FEB	1 ♓ 3 ♈	1 ♒ 16 ♓	1 ♐ 7 ♑	1 ♓ 12 ♈	1 ♑ 6 ♒	1 ♒	1 ♓ 25 ♈	1 ♑ 21 ♒
MAR	1 ♈ 15 ♉	1 ♓ 12 ♈	1 ♑ 5 ♒ 31 ♓	1 ♈ 8 ♉	1 ♒ 2 ♓ 26 ♈	1 ♒	1 ♈ 21 ♉	1 ♒ 16 ♓
APR	1 ♈	1 ♈ 5 ♉ 29 ♊	1 ♓ 25 ♈	1 ♉ 5 ♊	1 ♈ 19 ♉	1 ♒ 7 ♓	1 ♉ 15 ♊	1 ♓ 10 ♈
MAY	1 ♈	1 ♊ 24 ♋	1 ♈ 20 ♉	1 ♊ 9 ♋	1 ♉ 14 ♊	1 ♓ 6 ♈	1 ♊ 11 ♋	1 ♈ 4 ♉ 29 ♊
JUN	1 ♈ 6 ♉	1 ♋ 18 ♌	1 ♉ 14 ♊	1 ♋ 24 ♊	1 ♊ 7 ♋	1 ♈ 2 ♉ 27 ♊	1 ♋ 7 ♌	1 ♊ 22 ♋
JUL	1 ♉ 8 ♊	1 ♌ 14 ♍	1 ♊ 9 ♋	1 ♊	1 ♋ 2 ♌ 27 ♍	1 ♊ 22 ♋	1 ♌ 9 ♍	1 ♋ 16 ♌
AUG	1 ♊ 5 ♋ 31 ♌	1 ♍ 10 ♎	1 ♋ 2 ♌ 26 ♍	1 ♊ 5 ♋	1 ♍ 21 ♎	1 ♋ 16 ♌	1 ♍	1 ♌ 9 ♍
SEP	1 ♌ 25 ♍	1 ♎ 7 ♏	1 ♍ 19 ♎	1 ♋ 9 ♌	1 ♎ 15 ♏	1 ♌ 10 ♍	1 ♍ 21 ♌ 26 ♍	1 ♍ 3 ♎ 28 ♏
OCT	1 ♍ 19 ♎	1 ♏ 24 ♐ 28 ♏	1 ♎ 13 ♏	1 ♌ 7 ♍	1 ♏ 11 ♐	1 ♍ 3 ♎ 28 ♏	1 ♍	1 ♏ 22 ♐
NOV	1 ♎ 12 ♏	1 ♏	1 ♏ 6 ♐	1 ♎ 26 ♏	1 ♐ 6 ♑	1 ♏ 21 ♐	1 ♍ 10 ♎	1 ♐ 15 ♑
DEC	1 ♏ 6 ♐ 30 ♑	1 ♏	1 ♑ 25 ♒	1 ♏ 20 ♐	1 ♑ 7 ♒	1 ♐ 15 ♑	1 ♎ 8 ♏	1 ♑ 11 ♒

♀	1961	1962	1963	1964	1965	1966	1967	1968
JAN	1 ♒ 6 ♓	1 ♑ 22 ♒	1 ♏ 7 ♐	1 ♒ 17 ♓	1 ♐ 13 ♑	1 ♒	1 ♑ 7 ♒ 31 ♓	1 ♏ 2 ♐ 27 ♑
FEB	1 ♓ 3 ♈	1 ♒ 15 ♓	1 ♐ 6 ♑	1 ♓ 11 ♈	1 ♑ 6 ♒	1 ♒ 7 ♑ 26 ♒	1 ♓ 24 ♈	1 ♑ 21 ♒
MAR	1 ♈	1 ♓ 11 ♈	1 ♑ 5 ♒ 31 ♓	1 ♈ 8 ♉	1 ♒ 2 ♓ 26 ♈	1 ♒	1 ♈ 21 ♉	1 ♒ 16 ♓
APR	1 ♈	1 ♈ 4 ♉ 29 ♊	1 ♓ 25 ♈	1 ♉ 5 ♊	1 ♈ 19 ♉	1 ♒ 7 ♓	1 ♉ 15 ♊	1 ♓ 9 ♈
MAY	1 ♈	1 ♊ 24 ♋	1 ♈ 19 ♉	1 ♊ 10 ♋	1 ♉ 13 ♊	1 ♓ 6 ♈	1 ♊ 11 ♋	1 ♈ 4 ♉ 28 ♊
JUN	1 ♈ 6 ♉	1 ♋ 18 ♌	1 ♉ 13 ♊	1 ♋ 18 ♊	1 ♊ 7 ♋	1 ♉ 27 ♊	1 ♋ 7 ♌	1 ♊ 21 ♋
JUL	1 ♉ 8 ♊	1 ♌ 13 ♍	1 ♊ 8 ♋	1 ♊	1 ♌ 26 ♍	1 ♊ 22 ♋	1 ♌ 9 ♍	1 ♋ 16 ♌
AUG	1 ♊ 4 ♋ 30 ♌	1 ♍ 8 ♎	1 ♌ 26 ♍	1 ♊ 5 ♋	1 ♍ 20 ♎	1 ♋ 16 ♌	1 ♍	1 ♌ 9 ♍
SEP	1 ♌ 24 ♍	1 ♎ 8 ♏	1 ♍ 18 ♎	1 ♋ 9 ♌	1 ♎ 14 ♏	1 ♌ 9 ♍	1 ♍ 10 ♌	1 ♍ 3 ♎ 27 ♏
OCT	1 ♍ 18 ♎	1 ♏	1 ♎ 13 ♏	1 ♌ 6 ♍	1 ♏ 10 ♐	1 ♍ 3 ♎ 27 ♏	1 ♌ 2 ♍	1 ♏ 22 ♐
NOV	1 ♎ 12 ♏	1 ♏	1 ♏ 6 ♐ 30 ♑	1 ♎ 25 ♏	1 ♐ 6 ♑	1 ♏ 20 ♐	1 ♍ 10 ♎	1 ♐ 15 ♑
DEC	1 ♏ 6 ♐ 29 ♑	1 ♏	1 ♑ 24 ♒	1 ♏ 20 ♐	1 ♑ 8 ♒	1 ♐ 14 ♑	1 ♎ 8 ♏	1 ♑ 10 ♒

♀	1969	1970	1971	1972	1973	1974	1975	1976
JAN	1♒ 5♓	1♑ 22♒	1♏ 8♐	1♒ 17♓	1♐ 12♑	1♒ 30♑	1♑ 7♒ 31♓	1♏ 2♐ 27♑
FEB	1♓ 3♈	1♒ 15♓	1♐ 6♑	1♓ 11♈	1♑ 5♒	1♑	1♓ 24♈	1♑ 20♒
MAR	1♈	1♓ 11♈	1♑ 5♒ 30♓	1♈ 8♉	1♓ 25♈	1♒	1♈ 20♉	1♒ 15♓
APR	1♈	1♈ 4♉ 28♊	1♓ 24♈	1♉ 4♊	1♈ 19♉	1♒ 7♓	1♉ 14♊	1♓ 9♈
MAY	1♈	1♊ 23♋	1♈ 19♉	1♊ 11♋	1♉ 13♊	1♓ 5♈	1♊ 10♋	1♈ 3♉ 27♊
JUN	1♈ 6♉	1♋ 17♌	1♉ 13♊	1♋ 6♊	1♊ 8♋ 30♌	1♉ 26♊	1♋ 7♌	1♊ 21♋
JUL	1♉ 7♊	1♌ 13♍	1♊ 7♋	1♊	1♌ 26♍	1♊ 22♋	1♌ 10♍	1♋ 15♌
AUG	1♊ 4♋ 30♌	1♍ 9♎	1♌ 25♍	1♊ 7♋	1♍ 19♎	1♋ 15♌	1♍	1♌ 9♍
SEP	1♌ 24♍	1♎ 8♏	1♍ 18♎	1♋ 8♌	1♎ 14♏	1♌ 9♍	1♍ 3♌	1♍ 2♎ 26♏
OCT	1♍ 18♎	1♏	1♎ 12♏	1♌ 6♍ 31♎	1♏ 10♐	1♍ 3♎ 27♏	1♌ 5♍	1♏ 21♐
NOV	1♎ 11♏	1♏	1♏ 5♐ 30♑	1♎ 25♏	1♐ 6♑	1♏ 20♐	1♍ 10♎	1♐ 15♑
DEC	1♏ 5♐ 29♑	1♏	1♑ 24♒	1♏ 19♐	1♑ 8♒	1♐ 14♑	1♎ 7♏	1♑ 10♒

♀	1977	1978	1979	1980	1981	1982	1983	1984
JAN	1♒ 5♓	1♑ 21♒	1♏ 8♐	1♒ 16♓	1♐ 12♑	1♒ 24♑	1♑ 6♒ 30♓	1♏ 2♐ 26♑
FEB	1♓ 3♈	1♒ 14♓	1♐ 6♑	1♓ 10♈	1♑ 5♒ 28♓	1♑	1♓ 23♈	1♑ 20♒
MAR	1♈	1♓ 10♈	1♑ 4♒ 29♓	1♈ 7♉	1♓ 25♈	1♑ 3♒	1♈ 20♉	1♒ 15♓
APR	1♈	1♈ 3♉ 28♊	1♓ 23♈	1♉ 4♊	1♈ 18♉	1♒ 7♓	1♉ 14♊	1♓ 8♈
MAY	1♈	1♊ 22♋	1♈ 18♉	1♊ 13♋	1♉ 12♊	1♓ 5♈ 31♉	1♊ 10♋	1♈ 3♉ 27♊
JUN	1♈ 7♉	1♋ 17♌	1♉ 12♊	1♋ 6♊	1♊ 6♋ 30♌	1♉ 26♊	1♋ 7♌	1♊ 21♋
JUL	1♉ 7♊	1♌ 12♍	1♊ 7♋ 31♌	1♊	1♌ 25♍	1♊ 21♋	1♌ 11♍	1♋ 15♌
AUG	1♊ 3♋ 29♌	1♍ 8♎	1♌ 25♍	1♊ 7♋	1♍ 19♎	1♋ 15♌	1♍ 28♌	1♌ 8♍
SEP	1♌ 23♍	1♎ 8♏	1♍ 18♎	1♋ 8♌	1♎ 13♏	1♌ 8♍	1♌	1♍ 2♎ 26♏
OCT	1♍ 17♎	1♏	1♎ 12♏	1♌ 5♍ 31♎	1♏ 9♐	1♍ 2♎ 26♏	1♌ 6♍	1♏ 21♐
NOV	1♎ 11♏	1♏	1♏ 5♐ 29♑	1♎ 25♏	1♐ 6♑	1♏ 19♐	1♍ 10♎	1♐ 14♑
DEC	1♏ 4♐ 28♑	1♏	1♑ 23♒	1♏ 19♐	1♑ 9♒	1♐ 12♑	1♎ 7♏	1♑ 10♒

♀	1985	1986	1987	1988	1989	1990	1991	1992
JAN	1♒ 5♓	1♑ 21♒	1♏ 8♐	1♒ 16♓	1♐ 11♑	1♒ 17♑	1♑ 6♒ 30♓	1♐ 26♑
FEB	1♓ 3♈	1♒ 14♓	1♐ 6♑	1♓ 10♈	1♑ 4♒ 28♓	1♑	1♓ 23♈	1♑ 19♒
MAR	1♈	1♓ 9♈	1♑ 4♒ 29♓	1♈ 7♉	1♓ 24♈	1♑ 4♒	1♈ 19♉	1♒ 14♓
APR	1♈	1♈ 3♉ 27♊	1♓ 23♈	1♉ 4♊	1♈ 17♉	1♒ 7♓	1♉ 13♊	1♓ 7♈
MAY	1♈	1♊ 22♋	1♈ 18♉	1♊ 18♋ 27♊	1♉ 12♊	1♓ 4♈ 31♉	1♊ 9♋	1♈ 2♉ 26♊
JUN	1♈ 7♉	1♋ 16♌	1♉ 12♊	1♊	1♊ 5♋ 30♌	1♉ 25♊	1♋ 7♌	1♊ 20♋
JUL	1♉ 7♊	1♌ 12♍	1♊ 6♋ 31♌	1♊	1♌ 24♍	1♊ 20♋	1♌ 11♍	1♋ 14♌
AUG	1♊ 3♋ 28♌	1♍ 8♎	1♌ 24♍	1♊ 7♋	1♍ 18♎	1♋ 13♌	1♍ 22♌	1♌ 7♍
SEP	1♌ 23♍	1♎ 8♏	1♍ 17♎	1♋ 8♌	1♎ 13♏	1♌ 9♍	1♌	1♎ 25♏
OCT	1♍ 17♎	1♏	1♎ 11♏	1♌ 5♍ 30♎	1♏ 9♐	1♍ 2♎ 26♏	1♌ 7♍	1♏ 20♐
NOV	1♎ 10♏	1♏	1♏ 4♐ 28♑	1♎ 24♏	1♐ 6♑	1♏ 6♐	1♍ 9♎	1♐ 14♑
DEC	1♏ 4♐ 28♑	1♏	1♑ 23♒	1♏ 18♐	1♑ 10♒	1♐ 13♑	1♎ 7♏	1♑ 9♒

♀	1993	1994	1995	1996	1997	1998	1999	2000
JAN	1♒ 4♓	1♑ 20♒	1♏ 8♐	1♒ 15♓	1♐ 10♑	1♒ 10♑	1♑ 5♒ 29♓	1♐ 25♑
FEB	1♓ 3♈	1♒ 13♓	1♐ 5♑	1♓ 9♈	1♑ 4♒ 28♓	1♑	1♓ 22♈	1♑ 19♒
MAR	1♈	1♓ 9♈	1♑ 3♒ 29♓	1♈ 6♉	1♓ 24♈	1♑ 5♒	1♈ 19♉	1♒ 14♓
APR	1♈	1♈ 2♉ 27♊	1♓ 23♈	1♉ 4♊	1♈ 17♉	1♒ 7♓	1♉ 13♊	1♓ 7♈
MAY	1♈	1♊ 21♋	1♈ 17♉	1♊	1♉ 11♊	1♓ 4♈ 30♉	1♊ 9♋	1♈ 2♉ 26♊
JUN	1♈ 7♉	1♋ 15♌	1♉ 11♊	1♊	1♊ 4♋ 29♌	1♉ 25♊	1♋ 6♌	1♊ 19♋
JUL	1♉ 6♊	1♌ 12♍	1♊ 6♋ 30♌	1♊	1♌ 24♍	1♊ 20♋	1♌ 13♍	1♋ 14♌
AUG	1♊ 2♋ 28♌	1♍ 8♎	1♌ 23♍	1♊ 7♋	1♍ 18♎	1♋ 14♌	1♍ 16♌	1♌ 7♍
SEP	1♌ 22♍	1♎ 8♏	1♍ 17♎	1♋ 8♌	1♎ 12♏	1♌ 7♍	1♌	1♎ 25♏
OCT	1♍ 16♎	1♏	1♎ 11♏	1♌ 5♍ 30♎	1♏ 9♐	1♍ 2♎ 25♏	1♌ 8♍	1♏ 20♐
NOV	1♎ 9♏	1♏	1♏ 4♐ 28♑	1♎ 23♏	1♐ 6♑	1♏ 6♐	1♍ 10♎	1♐ 13♑
DEC	1♏ 3♐ 27♑	1♏	1♑ 22♒	1♏ 17♐	1♑ 12♒	1♐ 12♑	1♎ 6♏	1♑ 9♒

♂	1921	1922	1923	1924	1925	1926	1927	1928	1929	1930
JAN	1♒ 5♓	1♏	1♓ 21♈	1♏ 19♐	1♈	1♐	1♉	1♐ 19♑	1♊	1♑
FEB	1♓ 13♈	1♏ 18♐	1♈	1♐	1♈ 5♉	1♐ 9♑	1♉ 22♊	1♑ 28♒	1♊	1♑ 6♒
MAR	1♈ 25♉	1♐	1♈ 4♉	1♐ 6♑	1♉ 24♊	1♑ 23♒	1♊	1♒	1♊ 10♋	1♒ 17♓
APR	1♉	1♐	1♉ 16♊	1♑ 24♒	1♊	1♒	1♊ 17♋	1♒ 7♓	1♋	1♓ 24♈
MAY	1♉ 6♊	1♐	1♊ 30♋	1♒	1♊ 9♋	1♒ 3♓	1♋	1♓ 16♈	1♋ 13♌	1♈
JUN	1♊ 18♋	1♐	1♋	1♒ 24♓	1♋ 26♌	1♓ 15♈	1♋ 6♌	1♈ 26♉	1♌	1♈ 3♉
JUL	1♋	1♐	1♋ 16♌	1♓	1♌	1♈	1♌ 25♍	1♉	1♌ 4♍	1♉ 14♊
AUG	1♋ 3♌	1♐	1♌	1♓ 24♒	1♌ 12♍	1♉	1♍	1♉ 9♊	1♍ 21♎	1♊ 28♋
SEP	1♌ 19♍	1♐ 13♑	1♍	1♒	1♍ 28♎	1♉	1♍ 10♎	1♊	1♎	1♋
OCT	1♍	1♑ 30♒	1♍ 18♎	1♒ 19♓	1♎	1♉	1♎ 26♏	1♊ 3♋	1♎ 6♏	1♋ 20♌
NOV	1♍ 6♎	1♒	1♎	1♓	1♎ 13♏	1♉	1♏	1♋	1♏ 18♐	1♌
DEC	1♎ 26♏	1♒ 11♓	1♎ 4♏	1♓ 19♈	1♏ 28♐	1♉	1♏ 8♐	1♋ 20♊	1♐ 29♑	1♌

♂	1931	1932	1933	1934	1935	1936	1937	1938	1939	1940
JAN	1♌	1♑ 18♒	1♍	1♒	1♎	1♒ 14♓	1♎ 5♏	1♓ 30♈	1♏ 29♐	1♉ 4♊
FEB	1♌ 16♋	1♒ 25♓	1♍	1♒ 4♓	1♎	1♓ 22♈	1♏	1♈	1♐	1♊ 17♋
MAR	1♋ 30♌	1♓	1♍	1♓ 14♈	1♎	1♈	1♏ 13♐	1♈ 12♉	1♐ 21♑	1♋
APR	1♌	1♓ 3♈	1♍	1♈ 22♉	1♎	1♉	1♐	1♉ 23♊	1♑	1♌
MAY	1♌	1♈ 12♉	1♍	1♉	1♎	1♉ 13♊	1♐ 14♏	1♊	1♑ 25♒	1♌ 17♍
JUN	1♌ 10♍	1♉ 22♊	1♍	1♉ 2♊	1♎	1♊ 25♋	1♏	1♊ 7♋	1♒	1♍
JUL	1♍	1♊	1♍ 6♎	1♊ 15♋	1♎ 29♏	1♋	1♏	1♋ 22♌	1♒ 21♓	1♍ 3♎
AUG	1♎	1♊ 4♋	1♎ 26♏	1♋ 30♌	1♏	1♋ 10♌	1♏ 8♐	1♌	1♓	1♎ 19♏
SEP	1♎ 17♏	1♋ 20♌	1♏	1♌	1♏ 16♐	1♌ 26♍	1♐ 30♑	1♌ 7♍	1♓ 24♈	1♏
OCT	1♏ 30♐	1♌	1♏ 9♐	1♌ 18♍	1♐ 28♑	1♍	1♑	1♍ 25♎	1♈	1♏ 5♐
NOV	1♐	1♌ 13♍	1♐ 19♑	1♍	1♑	1♍ 14♎	1♑ 11♒	1♎	1♈ 19♉	1♐ 20♑
DEC	1♐ 10♑	1♍	1♑ 28♒	1♍ 11♎	1♑ 7♒	1♎	1♒ 21♓	1♎ 11♏	1♉	1♑

♂	1941	1942	1943	1944	1945	1946	1947	1948	1949	1950
JAN	1 ♏ 4 ♐	1 ♈ 11 ♉	1 ♐ 26 ♑	1 ♊	1 ♐ 5 ♑	1 ♋	1 ♑ 25 ♒	1 ♍	1 ♑ 4 ♒	1 ♎
FEB	1 ♐ 17 ♑	1 ♉	1 ♑	1 ♊	1 ♑ 14 ♒	1 ♋	1 ♒	1 ♍ 12 ♌	1 ♒ 11 ♓	1 ♎
MAR	1 ♑	1 ♉ 7 ♊	1 ♑ 8 ♒	1 ♊ 29 ♋	1 ♒ 25 ♓	1 ♋	1 ♒ 4 ♓	1 ♌	1 ♓ 21 ♈	1 ♎ 28 ♍
APR	1 ♑ 2 ♒	1 ♊ 26 ♋	1 ♒ 17 ♓	1 ♋	1 ♓	1 ♋ 22 ♌	1 ♓ 11 ♈	1 ♌	1 ♈ 30 ♉	1 ♍
MAY	1 ♒ 16 ♓	1 ♋	1 ♓ 27 ♈	1 ♋ 22 ♌	1 ♓ 3 ♈	1 ♌	1 ♈ 21 ♉	1 ♌ 18 ♍	1 ♉	1 ♍
JUN	1 ♓	1 ♋ 14 ♌	1 ♈	1 ♌	1 ♈ 11 ♉	1 ♌ 20 ♍	1 ♉	1 ♍	1 ♉ 10 ♊	1 ♍ 11 ♎
JUL	1 ♓ 2 ♈	1 ♌	1 ♈ 7 ♉	1 ♌ 12 ♍	1 ♉ 23 ♊	1 ♍	1 ♉ 17 ♊	1 ♍ 17 ♎	1 ♊ 23 ♋	1 ♎
AUG	1 ♈	1 ♍	1 ♉ 23 ♊	1 ♍ 29 ♎	1 ♊	1 ♍ 9 ♎	1 ♊ 13 ♋	1 ♎	1 ♋	1 ♎ 10 ♏
SEP	1 ♈	1 ♍ 17 ♎	1 ♊	1 ♎	1 ♊ 7 ♋	1 ♎ 24 ♏	1 ♋	1 ♎ 3 ♏	1 ♋ 7 ♌	1 ♏ 25 ♐
OCT	1 ♈	1 ♎	1 ♊	1 ♎ 13 ♏	1 ♋	1 ♏	1 ♌	1 ♏ 17 ♐	1 ♌ 27 ♍	1 ♐
NOV	1 ♈	1 ♎ 2 ♏	1 ♊	1 ♏ 25 ♐	1 ♋ 11 ♌	1 ♏ 6 ♐	1 ♌	1 ♐ 26 ♑	1 ♍	1 ♐ 6 ♑
DEC	1 ♈	1 ♏ 15 ♐	1 ♊	1 ♐	1 ♌ 26 ♋	1 ♐ 17 ♑	1 ♍	1 ♑	1 ♍ 26 ♎	1 ♑ 15 ♒

♂	1951	1952	1953	1954	1955	1956	1957	1958	1959	1960
JAN	1 ♒ 22 ♓	1 ♎ 20 ♏	1 ♓	1 ♏	1 ♓ 15 ♈	1 ♏ 14 ♐	1 ♈ 28 ♉	1 ♐	1 ♉	1 ♐ 14 ♑
FEB	1 ♓	1 ♏	1 ♓ 8 ♈	1 ♏ 9 ♐	1 ♈ 26 ♉	1 ♐ 28 ♑	1 ♉	1 ♐ 3 ♑	1 ♉ 10 ♊	1 ♑ 23 ♒
MAR	1 ♓ 2 ♈	1 ♏	1 ♈ 20 ♉	1 ♐	1 ♉	1 ♑	1 ♉ 17 ♊	1 ♑ 17 ♒	1 ♊	1 ♒
APR	1 ♈ 10 ♉	1 ♏	1 ♉	1 ♐ 12 ♑	1 ♉ 10 ♊	1 ♑ 14 ♒	1 ♊	1 ♒ 27 ♓	1 ♊ 10 ♋	1 ♒ 2 ♓
MAY	1 ♉ 21 ♊	1 ♏	1 ♊	1 ♑	1 ♊ 26 ♋	1 ♒	1 ♊ 4 ♋	1 ♓	1 ♋	1 ♓ 11 ♈
JUN	1 ♊	1 ♏	1 ♊ 14 ♋	1 ♑	1 ♋	1 ♒ 3 ♓	1 ♋ 21 ♌	1 ♓ 7 ♈	1 ♋ 20 ♌	1 ♈ 20 ♉
JUL	1 ♊ 3 ♋	1 ♏	1 ♋ 29 ♌	1 ♑	1 ♋ 11 ♌	1 ♓	1 ♌	1 ♈ 21 ♉	1 ♌ 20 ♍	1 ♉
AUG	1 ♋ 18 ♌	1 ♏ 27 ♐	1 ♌	1 ♑	1 ♌ 27 ♍	1 ♓	1 ♌ 8 ♍	1 ♉	1 ♍	1 ♉ 2 ♊
SEP	1 ♌	1 ♐	1 ♌ 14 ♍	1 ♑	1 ♍	1 ♓	1 ♍ 24 ♎	1 ♉ 21 ♊	1 ♍ 5 ♎	1 ♊ 21 ♋
OCT	1 ♌ 5 ♍	1 ♐ 12 ♑	1 ♍	1 ♑ 21 ♒	1 ♍ 13 ♎	1 ♓	1 ♎	1 ♊ 29 ♉	1 ♎ 21 ♏	1 ♋
NOV	1 ♍ 24 ♎	1 ♑ 21 ♒	1 ♍ 21 ♎	1 ♒	1 ♎ 29 ♏	1 ♓	1 ♎ 8 ♏	1 ♉	1 ♏	1 ♋
DEC	1 ♎	1 ♒ 30 ♓	1 ♎ 20 ♏	1 ♒ 4 ♓	1 ♏	1 ♓ 6 ♈	1 ♏ 23 ♐	1 ♉	1 ♏ 3 ♐	1 ♋

♂	1961	1962	1963	1964	1965	1966	1967	1968	1969	1970
JAN	1 ♋	1 ♑	1 ♌	1 ♑ 13 ♒	1 ♍	1 ♒ 30 ♓	1 ♎	1 ♒ 9 ♓	1 ♏	1 ♓ 24 ♈
FEB	1 ♋ 5 ♊ 7 ♋	1 ♑ 2 ♒	1 ♌	1 ♒ 20 ♓	1 ♍	1 ♓	1 ♎ 12 ♏	1 ♓ 17 ♈	1 ♏ 25 ♐	1 ♈
MAR	1 ♋	1 ♒ 12 ♓	1 ♌	1 ♓ 29 ♈	1 ♍	1 ♓ 9 ♈	1 ♏ 31 ♎	1 ♈ 28 ♉	1 ♐	1 ♈ 7 ♉
APR	1 ♋	1 ♓ 19 ♈	1 ♌	1 ♈	1 ♍	1 ♈ 17 ♉	1 ♎	1 ♉	1 ♐	1 ♉ 18 ♊
MAY	1 ♋ 6 ♌	1 ♈ 28 ♉	1 ♌	1 ♈ 7 ♉	1 ♍	1 ♉ 28 ♊	1 ♎	1 ♉ 8 ♊	1 ♐	1 ♊
JUN	1 ♌ 28 ♍	1 ♉	1 ♌ 3 ♍	1 ♉ 17 ♊	1 ♍ 29 ♎	1 ♊	1 ♎	1 ♊ 21 ♋	1 ♐	1 ♊ 2 ♋
JUL	1 ♍	1 ♉ 9 ♊	1 ♍ 27 ♎	1 ♊ 30 ♋	1 ♎	1 ♊ 11 ♋	1 ♎ 19 ♏	1 ♋	1 ♐	1 ♋ 18 ♌
AUG	1 ♍ 17 ♎	1 ♊ 22 ♋	1 ♎	1 ♋	1 ♎ 20 ♏	1 ♋ 25 ♌	1 ♏	1 ♋ 5 ♌	1 ♐	1 ♌
SEP	1 ♎	1 ♋	1 ♎ 12 ♏	1 ♋ 15 ♌	1 ♏	1 ♌	1 ♏ 10 ♐	1 ♌ 21 ♍	1 ♐ 21 ♑	1 ♌ 3 ♍
OCT	1 ♎ 2 ♏	1 ♋ 11 ♌	1 ♏ 25 ♐	1 ♌	1 ♏ 4 ♐	1 ♌ 12 ♍	1 ♐ 23 ♑	1 ♍	1 ♑	1 ♍ 20 ♎
NOV	1 ♏ 13 ♐	1 ♌	1 ♐	1 ♌ 6 ♍	1 ♐ 14 ♑	1 ♍	1 ♑	1 ♍ 9 ♎	1 ♑ 4 ♒	1 ♎
DEC	1 ♐ 24 ♑	1 ♌	1 ♐ 5 ♑	1 ♍	1 ♑ 23 ♒	1 ♍ 4 ♎	1 ♑ 2 ♒	1 ♎ 30 ♏	1 ♒ 15 ♓	1 ♎ 6 ♏

♂	1971	1972	1973	1974	1975	1976	1977	1978	1979	1980
JAN	1 ♏ 23 ♐	1 ♈	1 ♐	1 ♉	1 ♐ 21 ♑	1 ♊	1 ♑	1 ♌ 26 ♋	1 ♑ 21 ♒	1 ♍
FEB	1 ♐	1 ♈ 10 ♉	1 ♐ 12 ♑	1 ♉ 27 ♊	1 ♑	1 ♊	1 ♑ 9 ♒	1 ♋	1 ♒ 28 ♓	1 ♍
MAR	1 ♐ 12 ♑	1 ♉ 27 ♊	1 ♑ 27 ♒	1 ♊	1 ♑ 3 ♒	1 ♊ 18 ♋	1 ♒ 20 ♓	1 ♋	1 ♓	1 ♍ 12 ♌
APR	1 ♑	1 ♊	1 ♒	1 ♊ 20 ♋	1 ♒ 11 ♓	1 ♋	1 ♓ 28 ♈	1 ♋ 11 ♌	1 ♓ 7 ♈	1 ♌
MAY	1 ♑ 3 ♒	1 ♊ 12 ♋	1 ♒ 8 ♓	1 ♋	1 ♓ 21 ♈	1 ♋ 16 ♌	1 ♈	1 ♌	1 ♈ 16 ♉	1 ♌ 4 ♍
JUN	1 ♒	1 ♋ 28 ♌	1 ♓ 21 ♈	1 ♋ 9 ♌	1 ♈	1 ♌	1 ♈ 6 ♉	1 ♌ 14 ♍	1 ♉ 26 ♊	1 ♍
JUL	1 ♒	1 ♌	1 ♈	1 ♌ 27 ♍	1 ♉	1 ♌ 7 ♍	1 ♉ 18 ♊	1 ♍	1 ♊	1 ♍ 11 ♎
AUG	1 ♒	1 ♌ 15 ♍	1 ♈ 12 ♉	1 ♍	1 ♉ 14 ♊	1 ♍ 24 ♎	1 ♊	1 ♍ 4 ♎	1 ♊ 8 ♋	1 ♎ 29 ♏
SEP	1 ♒	1 ♍	1 ♉	1 ♍ 12 ♎	1 ♊	1 ♎	1 ♋	1 ♎ 20 ♏	1 ♋ 25 ♌	1 ♏
OCT	1 ♒	1 ♎	1 ♉ 30 ♈	1 ♎ 17 ♏	1 ♊ 17 ♋	1 ♎ 8 ♏	1 ♋ 27 ♌	1 ♏	1 ♌	1 ♏ 12 ♐
NOV	1 ♒ 6 ♓	1 ♎ 15 ♏	1 ♈	1 ♏	1 ♋ 26 ♊	1 ♏ 21 ♐	1 ♌	1 ♏ 2 ♐	1 ♌ 20 ♍	1 ♐ 22 ♑
DEC	1 ♓ 26 ♈	1 ♏ 30 ♐	1 ♈ 24 ♉	1 ♏ 11 ♐	1 ♊	1 ♐	1 ♌	1 ♐ 13 ♑	1 ♍	1 ♑ 31 ♒

♂	1981	1982	1983	1984	1985	1986	1987	1988	1989	1990
JAN	♒	♎	♒ 17 ♓	♎ 11 ♏	♓	♏	♓ 8 ♈	♏ 8 ♐	♈ 19 ♉	♐ 30 ♑
FEB	♒ 7 ♓	♎	♓ 25 ♈	♏	♓ 3 ♈	♏ 2 ♐	♈ 21 ♉	♐ 22 ♑	♉	♑
MAR	♓ 17 ♈	♎	♈	♏	♈ 15 ♉	♐ 28 ♑	♉	♑	♉ 11 ♊	♑ 12 ♒
APR	♈ 25 ♉	♎	♈ 5 ♉	♏	♉ 26 ♊	♑	♉ 6 ♊	♑ 7 ♒	♊ 29 ♋	♒ 21 ♓
MAY	♉	♎	♉ 17 ♊	♏	♊	♑	♊ 21 ♋	♒ 22 ♓	♋	♓ 31 ♈
JUN	♉ 5 ♊	♎	♋	♏	♊ 9 ♋	♑	♋	♓	♋ 17 ♌	♈
JUL	♊ 18 ♋	♎	♋	♏	♋ 25 ♌	♑	♋ 7 ♌	♓ 14 ♈	♌	♈ 13 ♉
AUG	♋	♎ 3 ♏	♋ 14 ♌	♏ 17 ♐	♌	♑	♌ 23 ♍	♈	♌ 3 ♍	♉ 31 ♊
SEP	♋ 2 ♌	♏ 20 ♐	♌ 30 ♍	♐	♌ 10 ♍	♑	♍	♈	♍ 20 ♎	♊
OCT	♌ 21 ♍	♐ 31 ♑	♍	♐ 5 ♑	♍ 28 ♎	♑ 9 ♒	♍ 8 ♎	♈ 24 ♓	♎	♊
NOV	♍	♑	♍ 18 ♎	♑ 16 ♒	♎	♒ 26 ♓	♎ 24 ♏	♓ 26 ♈	♎ 4 ♏	♊
DEC	♍ 16 ♎	♑ 10 ♒	♎	♒ 25 ♓	♎ 15 ♏	♓	♏	♈	♏ 18 ♐	♊ 14 ♉

♂	1991	1992	1993	1994	1995	1996	1997	1998	1999	2000
JAN	♉ 21 ♊	♐ 9 ♑	♋	♑ 28 ♒	♍ 23 ♌	♑ 9 ♒	♍ 3 ♎	♒ 25 ♓	♎ 26 ♏	♒ 4 ♓
FEB	♊	♑ 18 ♒	♋	♒	♌	♒ 15 ♓	♎	♓	♏	♓ 12 ♈
MAR	♊	♒ 28 ♓	♋	♒ 7 ♓	♌	♓ 25 ♈	♎ 8 ♍	♓ 5 ♈	♏	♈ 23 ♉
APR	♊ 3 ♋	♓	♋ 28 ♌	♓ 15 ♈	♌	♈	♍	♈ 13 ♉	♏	♉
MAY	♋ 27 ♌	♓ 6 ♈	♌	♈ 24 ♉	♌ 26 ♍	♈ 3 ♉	♍	♉ 24 ♊	♏ 6 ♎	♉ 4 ♊
JUN	♌	♈ 15 ♉	♌ 23 ♍	♉	♍	♉ 12 ♊	♍ 19 ♎	♊	♎	♊ 16 ♋
JUL	♌ 16 ♍	♉ 27 ♊	♍	♉ 4 ♊	♍ 21 ♎	♊ 26 ♋	♎	♊ 6 ♋	♎ 5 ♏	♋
AUG	♍	♊	♍ 12 ♎	♊ 17 ♋	♎	♋	♎ 14 ♏	♋ 21 ♌	♏	♌
SEP	♎	♊ 12 ♋	♎ 27 ♏	♋	♎ 7 ♏	♋ 10 ♌	♏ 28 ♐	♌	♏ 3 ♐	♌ 17 ♍
OCT	♎ 16 ♏	♋	♏	♋ 5 ♌	♏ 20 ♐	♌ 30 ♍	♐	♌ 7 ♍	♐ 17 ♑	♍
NOV	♏ 29 ♐	♋	♏ 9 ♐	♌	♐	♍	♐ 9 ♑	♍ 27 ♎	♑ 26 ♒	♍ 4 ♎
DEC	♐	♋	♐ 20 ♑	♌ 12 ♍	♑	♍	♑ 18 ♒	♎	♒	♎ 23 ♏